—SCIENCE—
THROUGH THE
—SEASONS—

WINTER
ON THE FARM

Janet Fitzgerald

Hamish Hamilton · London

Acknowledgement
I should like to express my gratitude to the schools,
teachers and children with whom I have worked, and
with whose help I have gained the experience and con-
fidence needed to write this series. I am particularly
indebted to those schools which allowed photographs
to be taken as the children carried out their investigations. Thanks are also due to Chris Fairclough for
some of the excellent photographs illustrating the
texts.

Janet Fitzgerald

The publishers would like to thank the following for
supplying photographs for this book:

Ardea 19 (left and right); Bruce Coleman front cover,
14; Chris Fairclough back cover; 9–11, 13, 15–18, 21–
23, 25; Farmer's Weekly 8, 12, 24, 26, 27; NHPA title
page 20.

Author's note

Books in this series are intended for use by young children actively engaged in exploring the environment in the company of a teacher or parent. Many lifelong interests are formed at this early age, and a caring attitude towards plants, animals and resources can be nurtured to become a mature concern for conservation in general.

The basis for all scientific investigation rests on the ability to observe closely and to ask questions. These books aim to increase a child's awareness so that he or she learns to make accurate observations. First-hand experience is encouraged and simple investigations of observations are suggested. The child will suggest many more! The aim is to give children a broad base of experience and 'memories' on which to build for the future.

HAMISH HAMILTON CHILDREN'S BOOKS

Published by the Penguin Group
27 Wrights Lane, London W8 5TZ, England
Viking Penguin Inc, 40 West 23rd Street, New York, New York 10010, U.S.A.
Penguin Books Australia Ltd, Ringwood, Victoria, Australia
Penguin Books Canada Ltd, 2801 John Street, Markham, Ontario, Canada L3R 1B4
Penguin Books (N.Z.) Ltd, 182–190 Wairau Road, Auckland 10, New Zealand

Penguin Books Ltd, Registered Offices: Harmondsworth, Middlesex, England

First published in Great Britain 1989 by
Hamish Hamilton Children's Books

Copyright © 1989 by Janet Fitzgerald

1 3 5 7 9 10 8 6 4 2

British Library Cataloguing in Publication Data
Fitzgerald, Janet
   Winter on the farm.
   1. Agricultural industries. Farms – For
   children
   I. Title II. Series
   338.1
   ISBN 0–241–12579–0

Printed in Great Britain by William Clowes Ltd, Beccles & London

Contents

It is winter on the farm and cows are kept indoors.

The cows live in the barn in winter.

Who will visit them every day
and bring food?

Where will the cows sleep?

We must take care of our animals in winter.
They must not get cold.

our quinea pig is

Choose a good place for your pet cage.
Make sure it will be warm and comfortable.
Will it be quiet and undisturbed?

It is winter on the farm and the farmer collects bedding for the animals.

Why do the animals need bedding?

Where did the bedding come from?

Guinea pigs like wood chippings
and dried grass for bedding.

Squeeze the bedding in your hands.

How does it feel?

If the bedding gets wet
how long does it take to dry?

We must make sure that the
guinea pig has dry bedding.

It is winter on the farm and there are sheep on the hillside.

The sheep stay outside
even when it is very cold.

How do the sheep keep warm?

How will the sheep get food?

When winter comes
what sort of coat
do you wear?

Look to see what your
friends are wearing.

Collect some
pieces of fabric.

Feel the fabric and
look at it carefully.

Sort out the fabrics
you think would
keep you warm.

11

It is winter on the farm and

hens lay eggs

Can you see where the hens will lay their eggs?

How will the hens make themselves comfortable?

Ask an adult to buy
six eggs for you.

Are they all
the same size?

Are they the
same colour?

Break one of the eggs
into a dish.

Look closely at
the different parts
of the egg.

It is winter on the farm and fences are mended.

How are the fences made?

Why does the farmer need strong fences?

Is winter a good time to mend fences?

Go for a walk near to your home or school.

Look to see how people fence their gardens.

Draw all the different fences you see.

Which kind of fence do most people choose?

It is winter on the farm and hedges are trimmed.

Look at the patterns the farmer is making in the hedge.

Why does the farmer trim the hedge?

What has happened to the birds and insects that live in the hedge?

If you have a hedge in your garden
or school, go to look at it in winter.

Look to see if anything is growing there.

Are there any signs of animals living there?

Are there any berries or other fruits?

It is winter on the farm and
holly is collected for decoration.

Is holly easy to see in winter?

Why does holly make good decorations?

What colour are the holly berries?

Carefully collect a few sprigs of holly.

Choose different colours if you can.

Look at two holly leaves to see if they are the same.

Do they feel the same?

Are they the same colour?

Count the prickles on ten holly leaves.

Make a chart to show what you find.

It is winter on the farm and ivy makes a good hiding place

Why does ivy make a good hiding place?

How do birds keep warm in winter?

What can we do to help birds in winter?

Ivy often grows on the side of buildings.
See if you can find some.
Collect a few leaves.

Look at the shapes of the ivy leaves.
How many shapes have you collected?
Mix paint to make the colour of the leaves.
Make a picture to show the shapes.

It is winter on the farm and
there is ice on the pond.

Is all the pond covered with ice?

Where have the birds found to swim?

What will the ducks find to eat?

On a frosty morning
look for icicles.

Where are most
of them hanging?

Take an icicle indoors.

Put it into a dish.

Watch to see what
happens to the icicle.

Make a drawing
of the icicle
when you bring it in.

How does it change?

It is winter on the farm and the farmer makes plans.

The farmer must decide what to grow next year.

He may need to buy new machinery.

How will the farmer find out
about all the new things?

Ask if you can have a small plot of land to make into a garden.

Decide what sort of things you want to grow in your garden.

Will it be flowers, vegetables or herbs?

Make a plan to show what you will grow in your garden.

Looking at . . .

. . . buildings on the farm

If you go to a farm
you will see lots of
different buildings.

What do you think these buildings are for?

Try to find out about other farm buildings.

For teachers and parents

We all recognise that children possess an insatiable curiosity about the rich environment and exciting experiences around them. For this reason they have a natural affinity for science and a basic inclination to explore and discover the world in which we live. We need to foster this sense of wonder by encouraging a scientific way of thinking in the early years. Children's own experience of the immediate environment will provide a natural starting point.

Through science children can evolve an active process of enquiry. This begins with observation (including sorting, comparing, ordering and measuring) and continues with asking questions, devising practical investigations, predicting outcomes, controlling variables, noting results, and perhaps modifying the original question in the light of discovery. The books in this series offer suggestions for engaging young children in this sort of active enquiry by relating seasonal change to familiar surroundings.

Extension activities

Pages 6–7
Study the behaviour of an animal over several months and keep a diary. Does temperature or time of day make a difference to the animal's behaviour? When does he move around most? When does he sleep, eat, drink or play? How much food does he need for a day, week or month? Devise a comfortable method of weighing the animal and keep a record of gains and losses. Investigate the animal's response to dark, light, sound or strong smells.

Pages 8–9
Compare nests made from different materials. Consider preferences e.g. cats and dogs like soft woollen blankets. The hedgerow in winter might reveal nests and other habitats. If an abandoned nest is removed make sure it is free from invertebrates

Study the way a guinea pig makes its nest. Does it take all the wood chippings to one end? Does it use any other material in the nest?

Pages 10–11

Extend the investigations into the insulating properties of material. Fill washing-up liquid bottles with the same amount of hot water, wrap in fabrics and record heat retention either by feeling or measuring with a simple thermometer. Compare the fabrics. Do the best insulators have closer weaves or are they thicker, heavier or lighter? Does the colour make a difference?

Pages 12–13

Make a survey of favourite ways of eating eggs (e.g. scrambled, fried, boiled or poached). Try different recipes. Add colours to the shells to decorate. Consider the eggs of other species, such as frog and toad spawn, snails, butterflies, fish. Emphasise the concept of a life cycle.

Pages 14–15

Consider the fences used on a farm. For what purposes do most people use fences? Are they for keeping things out or keeping things in? Investigate the materials used for fences. Which are natural and which man made? Are fences all made in the same way and from the same materials? Do all fences have gates in them somewhere?

Pages 16–17

Look at the different layers of the hedge: the field or verge, the bottom of the hedge, the shrub layer and the tree layer. Look for evidence of different plants and animals. Look for tracks and signs at the bottom of the hedge, prints, acorns, snails' shells, beech nuts, berries or litter. Look for toadstools, holly, ivy and other evergreens. Study the hedgerow at different times of the year.

Pages 18–19

Compare holly with other evergreens. Look at size, shape and colour of leaves; distribution on the twig and colour of bark. Look for evidence of bird perches in evergreens. Investigate the holly berries. Where do they grow on the holly twig? Are they growing singly or in groups? What shape are the berries? Dissect a berry and look at the seeds. Look for seedlings around the holly bush and measure the distance from the parent tree. Plant some holly seeds.

Pages 20–21
Discover the places where ivy grows
easily and try to suggest reasons.
Examine the stem of the ivy and the way
the plant attaches itself to trees etc. Look
for evidence of animals living in the ivy
e.g. remains of spiders' webs, chrysalids,
bird droppings. Some ivy will have
berries and winter flowers.

Pages 22–23
Examine puddles covered with ice.
Where does the ice begin to melt? What
happens to the ice as it melts? Once the
ice has melted is the puddle bigger or
smaller? Look at icicles to see if they are
smooth, even and all the same shape.
How are different shapes produced? How
long does it take an icicle to melt?
Measure the amount of water from
different icicles. Does it relate to size?

Pages 24–25
Collect farm magazines and catalogues.
Look to see what the farmer will be doing
at different times of the year. Work out a
sequence of events e.g. if seeds are to be
sown what must first be done to the soil?
Try to find out when the seeds are to be
sown, at what depth and how far apart.
How does the farmer know how much
seed he will need for a big field? Once the
seeds are sown what must the farmer do?
What happens about weeds? Compare
with what we can do about weeds in the
garden.

Index